Honey:

The Natural Miracle Healing Substance: Facts about the wonder that is honey with recipes for Natural Remedies, Skin and Beauty

Disclaimer

Although the author and publisher have made every effort to ensure that the information in this book was correct at press time, the author and publisher do not assume and hereby disclaim any liability to any party for any loss, injury, damage or disruption caused by errors or omissions, whether such errors or omissions result from negligence, accident, non-functional websites, or any other cause. Any advice or strategy contained herein may not be suitable for every individual.

Table of Contents

Introduction

Honey is the sticky sweet substance produced by bees from the nectar of flowering plants. Not only can honey be used as a natural sweetener for your favorite recipes, but it can also be used medicinally. In fact, honey has been a key ingredient in natural remedies for common ailments for thousands of years. Ancient cave paintings found in Spain suggest that humans have been gathering and using honey for at least 8,000 years – possibly more. Today, honey is making a comeback in herbal remedies as a treatment for everything from the common cold to gastric disturbances and even external wounds.

In this book you will learn the basics about this magical healing substance including a history of its use, its benefits as an herbal remedy, and a collection of recipes using honey. By the time you finish this book you will be eager to stock your pantry with honey and you will find yourself using it more and more often in your everyday life. What are you waiting for? Start reading to learn the benefits of this wonderful substance!

Chapter One: All About Honey

Honey is an all-natural substance that has been around for as long as bees and flowers. It is unknown exactly how long humans have been using honey, but evidence suggests that it has been a common ingredient for both culinary and medicinal applications for several thousand years. In this section you will receive specific information about the background and historical use of honey.

Background and History of Use

As it has already been mentioned, some of the earliest evidence linking humans and honey comes from ancient cave paintings found in Spain. These cave paintings date back to 7,000 BC and they may be the earliest documentation of beekeeping by humans. Fossil evidence suggests, however, that bees have been producing honey for well over 150 million years – long before humans ever walked the earth. Honey has played a significant role in a variety of ancient civilizations, including Egyptian, Greek, and Roman civilizations. <u>Below you will find an overview of the use of honey in several ancient civilizations</u>:

1. The oldest remains of honey were found in Georgia, dating back more than 5,000 years ago. These remains were found on clay vessels – it was common in ancient Georgia for honey to be packed for an individual's journey to the afterlife.

2. In ancient Egypt, honey was sacred – the bee was a symbol of royalty and honey was often given as a gift to the gods. Ancient Egyptians also used honey as a sweetener and as an ingredient in embalming fluid.

3. The ancient Greeks recognized both the culinary and medicinal importance of honey – it was widely used as a sweetener for cakes and sweetmeats. The Greeks also used honey to make cakes that were offered to the gods.

4. The ancient Romans used honey extensively in cooking and gave it as a gift to the gods – beekeeping flourished throughout the duration of the Roman Empire.

5. With the rise of Christianity, the demand for honey rose as well – both beeswax and honey were used to create church candles.

6. The importance of honey in Europe continued well into the Renaissance until sugar arrived. Up until the 17th century, honey was used just as frequently as sugar but then its use began to decline.

7. Honey is one of the five elixirs of immortality (Panchamrita) in the Hindu religion – it is poured over deities in temples as part of a ritual called Madhu abhisheka.

8. In the Jewish tradition, honey is a symbol of the New Year, Rosh Hashanah. A traditional meal for this holiday consists of apple slices dipped in honey. Straws of honey are also a common gift given to children to usher in the New Year.

Chapter Two: Benefits of Honey

The fact that humans have been gathering and using honey for more than 8,000 years is enough to suggest that it is something important. Not only is honey used for culinary purposes as a sweetening agent, but it also plays an important role in traditional medicine and herbal remedies. Below you will find a list of some of the many benefits provided by honey:

1. Honey has natural antibacterial and antiseptic properties which make it beneficial for cleaning and healing wounds – it can also be applied to wounds to keep scabs from sticking to the bandage.

2. In laboratory studies, honey has been found to kill cancer cells – its efficacy as a cancer treatment for humans is still being studied.

3. There is some evidence to suggest that honey can help to treat minor burns when used in the dressing for the wound.

4. A herbal remedy including honey and warm lemon water has long been recommended as a treatment for cold and cough.

5. When applied topically, honey can help to moisturize dry and damaged skin in an all-natural way.

6. Medicinally, honey may be beneficial for the prevention of heart disease by helping to improve blood flow and preventing damage to the capillaries.

7. The antibacterial properties of honey can help to destroy the bacteria that causes acne, it may also help to prevent scarring.

8. When applied to wounds, honey helps to soothe and disinfect while also reducing pain and inflammation – it may help speed healing as well.

9. Manuka honey, a type of honey produced in New Zealand, has been used to treat pressure sores and chronic leg ulcers.

10. Certain laboratory studies suggest that honey might be beneficial for clearing stuffy noses and easing pollen-related allergies.

11. In a clinical study, honey was shown to be more beneficial than dextromethorphan (a common cough suppressant) in relieving nighttime cough in children.

12. Cough syrups containing honey help to soothe the membranes in the esophagus while also fighting infection to help reduce the duration of the illness.

Note: Though honey is all-natural and considered safe for human consumption, it should never be given to a child under 1 year of age. Honey can carry the spores responsible for botulism and infants do not have sufficiently developed immune system to protect them against the disease.

Chapter Three: Natural Recipes Using Honey

As you know by now, honey can be used for a wide variety of things, both culinary and medicinal. Honey has played and continues to play an important role in herbal medicine, as you will see in the recipes provided in this chapter. In the following pages you will find a collection of recipes for skin and beauty products made with honey as well as various natural remedies for common illnesses. All recipes call for raw natural honey, not the processed jars of honey that have been heated to high temperatures to get the golden look.

Margaux J. Rathbun, a Certified Nutritional Therapy practitioner, explained why raw honey is so great for our bodies:

Just like most foods that are processed or pasteurized, liquid honey loses a lot of its beneficial nutrients when it undergoes a heating process. Raw honey is loaded with nutrients like energizing B vitamins and immune-boosting vitamin C. It contains antibacterial and antioxidant properties, helping fight off free radicals in your body and keeping your immune system strong. www.blisstree.com

Skin and Beauty

<u>Recipes Included in this Section</u>:

Mask for Normal Skin

Mask for Dry Skin

Mask for Oily Skin

Honey Lemon Facial Hair Remover

Honey-Cucumber Skin Toner

Honey Oat Facial Scrub

Brown Sugar Honey Scrub

Lemon Honey Sugar Scrub

Honey Vinegar Conditioner for Shine

Honey Olive Oil Conditioner for Moisture

Honey Rub for Hair Growth

Leave-in Conditioner with Honey

Mask for Normal Skin

This mask for normal skin is incredibly easy to prepare – all you need is honey and an apple! Use this mask once a week for the best results.

Ingredients:

1 medium apple, cored

2 tablespoons raw honey

Instructions:

1. Cut the apple into large pieces and place them in a food processor.
2. Pulse the apple until finely chopped.
3. Add the honey and blend until smooth.
4. Chill the mixture in the refrigerator for 10 minutes.
5. Pat the mixture into your face, lightly tapping it on with your fingers until it feels tacky.
6. Leave on for 30 minutes then rinse with warm water.

Mask for Dry Skin

This honey mask is designed for dry skin, though it has the added benefit of being good for anti-aging. Use this mask once a week for the best results.

Ingredients:

2 tablespoons chopped avocado

2 tablespoons raw honey

1 large egg yolk, raw

Instructions:

1. Place the avocado in a food processor or blender.
2. Add the honey and egg yolk and blend until smooth and well combined.
3. Spread the mask over your face and neck by hand.
4. Leave on for 30 minutes at least then rinse with warm water.

Mask for Oily Skin

This mask is designed for oily skin but it provides a number of additional benefits. Not only will this mask cleanse and moisturize your skin but it will also help to heal blemishes and draw impurities out of your skin for better clarity.

Ingredients:

1/3 cup chopped papaya

1/3 cup unsweetened cocoa powder

¼ cup raw honey

1 tablespoons heavy cream

1 tablespoon ground oats

Instructions:

1. Combine all of the ingredients in a food processor.
2. Pulse several times to combine then blend smooth.
3. As an alternative, stir together the ingredients by hand.
4. Spread the mixture in a thin layer on your face and neck.
5. Leave on for 10 minutes then rinse with warm water.

Honey Lemon Facial Hair Remover

If you are tired of shaving or bleaching your facial hair, this natural remedy is both gentle and effective. Made with natural ingredients like honey and lemon, this facial hair remover is the only recipe you will ever need.

Ingredients:

1 tablespoon raw honey

½ tablespoon ground oats

3 to 5 drops fresh lemon juice

Instructions:

1. Stir together the ingredients in a small bowl to form a paste.
2. Spread the paste on your face like you would apply a mask.
3. Leave the paste on for 15 minutes then rinse with warm water.
4. Repeat 2 to 3 times per week for 3 to 4 weeks.

Honey-Cucumber Facial Toner

This honey-cucumber facial toner is a gentle and natural way to hydrate your skin. Use this toner daily to give your skin a heathy glow.

Ingredients:

1 medium seedless cucumber

2 teaspoons raw honey

Instructions:

1. Peel and chop the cucumber then puree it in a food processor.
2. Strain the cucumber through fine mesh or cheesecloth and collect the juice.
3. Stir the honey into the juice then transfer the mixture to a small bottle.
4. Apply the toner to clean skin using a cotton ball in the morning and in the evening.
5. Let the mixture air dry then rinse with warm water.
6. Store the bottle in the refrigerator for 1 week.

Honey Oat Facial Scrub

This honey oat facial scrub is gentle on even the most sensitive skin but powerful enough to exfoliate your skin, leaving it feeling clean and smooth. Use this scrub daily for the best results.

Ingredients:

2 tablespoons dry oatmeal

1 tablespoon almond flour

1 tablespoon raw honey

½ teaspoon fresh lemon juice

Instructions:

1. Combine the ingredients in a small bowl.
2. Stir until it forms a thick paste.
3. Massage the mixture into damp skin for 2 minutes.
4. Rinse well with warm water then pat dry.

Brown Sugar Honey Scrub

This brown sugar honey scrub is better than anything you can buy at the store and, best of all, it is inexpensive to make! Use this scrub daily for the best results.

Ingredients:

2 tablespoons raw honey

2 tablespoons dark brown sugar

Instructions:

1. Combine the ingredients in a small bowl and stir well.
2. Wash your face then apply about ½ teaspoon of the mixture to damp skin.
3. Massage the scrub into your face in a circular motion for 1 minute.
4. Rinse well with warm water then pat dry.
5. Store the extra in an air-tight container at room temperature.

Lemon Honey Sugar Scrub

This lemon honey sugar scrub is fragrant and luxurious – best of all, it really works! Feel free to customize this recipe by swapping out the essential oils for a fragrance you prefer – try rose essential oil for a floral scent or orange essential oil for a citrus blend.

Ingredients:

1 cup coarse cane sugar

¼ cup extra-virgin olive oil

2 tablespoons raw honey

1 ½ teaspoon dried rosemary

12 drops lavender essential oil

12 drops lemon essential oil

Instructions:

1. Combine the sugar, rosemary, olive oil and honey in a bowl.
2. Stir until smooth and well combined.
3. Add the essential oils and stir well.
4. Wash your face then apply about ½ teaspoon of the mixture to damp skin.
5. Massage the scrub into your face in a circular motion for 1 minute.
6. Rinse well with warm water then pat dry.
7. Store the mixture in a glass jar with a lid at room temperature.

Honey Vinegar Conditioner for Shine

If you are looking for an all-natural conditioner that will leave your hair shiny and smooth, look no further than this recipe. Why spend a small fortune at the salon when the solution is right in your kitchen cupboard?

Ingredients:

½ cup plus 2 tablespoons apple cider vinegar

¼ cup raw honey

Instructions:

1. Stir together the ingredients in a small bowl until smooth.
2. Wash your hair in the shower as you normally wound.
3. Apply the mixture to damp hair and work it in by hand.
4. Let the conditioner sit for 15 minutes then rinse with warm water.

Honey Olive Oil Conditioner for Moisture

This homemade conditioner is all-natural and safe for even the driest, most damaged hair. Simply apply this conditioner 3 to 4 times a week for smooth, healthy hair.

Ingredients:

½ cup raw honey

¼ cup extra-virgin olive oil

Instructions:

1. Stir together the ingredients in a small bowl until smooth.
2. If needed, warm the mixture in the microwave for 10 seconds.
3. Wash your hair in the shower as you normally wound.
4. Apply the mixture to damp hair and work it in by hand.
5. Let the conditioner sit for 15 minutes then rinse with warm water.

Honey Rub for Hair Growth

If you want thicker, fuller hair, this honey rub is one recipe you have got to try. All it takes is a little honey and water once a week!

Ingredients:

½ cup plus 1 tablespoon raw honey

1 tablespoon warm water

Instructions:

1. Combine the ingredients in a bowl and stir well.
2. Pour the mixture onto your hair and work it into your scalp.
3. Massage the rub into your hair for 2 to 3 minutes.
4. Leave the mixture on your hair for 2 to 3 hours then rinse with warm water.
5. Repeat the treatment once a week.

Leave-in Conditioner with Honey

This leave-in conditioner is so easy to prepare that you will never buy a commercial leave-in conditioner again. Simply combine a little honey and warm water and apply it to your damp hair after every shower.

Ingredients:

4 cups warm water

1 teaspoon raw honey

Instructions:

1. Wash your hair in the shower as you normally would.
2. Stir together the water and honey and pour through your hair.
3. Wring out the extra liquid and let your hair dry naturally.

Natural Remedies

Recipes Included in this Section:

Honey Vinegar Drink for Acid Reflux

Insect Bite Treatment

Honey Treatment for Sinus Problems

Honey Hiccup-Stopper

Fever-Reducing Honey Tea

Honey Coconut Cough Syrup

Hot Toddy for Cold and Congestion

Honey Lemon Ginger Tea for Flu

Honey Vinegar Drink for Acid Reflux

Acid reflux, also known as gastroesophageal reflux (GERD), is very common, caused by the excessive production of stomach acid. This honey vinegar drink is a gentle and all-natural way to soothe the burning sensation you experience in your throat as a result of acid reflux.

Ingredients:

8 ounces hot water

1 tablespoon raw honey

1 tablespoon raw apple cider vinegar

Instructions:

1. Stir the honey and vinegar into the hot water.
2. Drink the beverage daily to soothe the throat and to prevent reflux.

Insect Bite Treatment

Insect bites can be a hassle to deal with – not only do they itch, but the resulting inflammation and irritation can also be painful. Rather than subjecting your damaged skin to chemical-laden commercial treatments, try a little honey!

Ingredients:

Raw honey, as needed

Light gauze bandage

Instructions:

1. Wash the area thoroughly and pat dry.
2. Spread a small amount of honey onto the wound.
3. Cover lightly with gauze. Re-dress the wound twice daily.

Honey Treatment for Sinus Problems

Whether you are plagued by sinus pressure, excessive sneezing, or a persistently runny nose, this honey treatment for sinus problems is just what you need. When taken consistently, this treatment can help to reduce the frequency of sinus problems.

Ingredients:

1 tablespoon raw honey

Instructions:

1. Take the honey by mouth at bedtime.
2. Repeat daily to reduce the occurrence of sinus problems.

Honey Hiccup-Stopper

Having a case of the hiccups can turn from funny to painful if it lasts too long. If holding your breath doesn't work, try this easy honey hiccup-stopper. It may not taste good, but it is sure to work!

Ingredients:

1 teaspoon raw honey

1 teaspoon castor oil

Instructions:

1. Stir together the ingredients in a small bowl.
2. Dip your finger into the mixture and lick it off.
3. Repeat every 10 minutes until your hiccups stop.

Fever-Reducing Honey Tea

This fever-reducing tea is a gentle and all-natural way to relieve even the most stubborn of fevers. Add more honey to taste, if needed, and drink two to three times daily until your fever dissipates.

Ingredients:

8 ounces hot water

1 teaspoon holy basil

1 teaspoon raw honey

¼ teaspoon fresh ground pepper

Instructions:

1. Combine the basil and water and let it steep for 5 minutes.
2. Stir in the black pepper and honey.
3. Sip the tea two to three times daily until your fever is gone.

Honey Coconut Cough Syrup

Store-bought cough syrups are made with all kinds of artificial ingredients that can do your body more harm than good. If you are looking for an all-natural remedy to soothe your aching throat, try this honey coconut cough syrup.

Ingredients:

¼ cup raw honey

2 tablespoons coconut oil

2 ½ tablespoons fresh lemon juice

Instructions:

1. Melt the coconut oil in a double boiler over low heat.
2. Stir in the honey and lemon juice until well combined.
3. Take 1 tablespoon of the warm syrup by mouth as desired.
4. As an alternative, stir the syrup into hot water or tea.
5. Store the extra in a glass container with a lid in the refrigerator.
6. To rewarm the syrup for use, place the jar in a bowl of hot water to soften.

Hot Toddy for Cold and Congestion

A nice hot toddy is the ultimate soothing beverage if you are feeling congested. Simply whip up a hot toddy when you feel a cold coming on and settle down for a healing nap.

Ingredients:

1 tbsp raw honey

1 shot (1/8 cup / 35ml) whiskey (more or less to your taste)

¼ cup fresh lemon juice

¼ - ½ cup boiling water (depending on size of glass / mug)

4-5 cloves

Slice of lemon

Instructions:

1. Combine the first 4 ingredients in an Irish coffee glass or mug stirring well to combine.
2. Pierce the slice of lemon with the cloves and add to the mug.
3. If the toddy is too strong, add more boiling water.
4. To treat congestion or sore throat, use bourbon whiskey.

Honey Lemon Ginger Tea for Flu

This honey lemon ginger mixture is something you definitely want to have on hand during cold and flu season. Prepare this mixture ahead of time and stir a teaspoon or so into a cup of hot water for a healing tea.

Ingredients:

2 medium lemons

2 inches fresh ginger

Raw honey, as needed

Glass jar with lid

Instructions:

1. Slice the lemons and the ginger.
2. Combine the lemons and ginger in the glass jar.
3. Pour the honey into the jar, allowing it to fill in the gaps between the lemon and ginger.
4. Add enough honey to fill the jar then cover tightly with the lid.
5. Store the jar in the refrigerator for at least 1 week.
6. Over time, the mixture will turn into a jelly.
7. When needed, stir 2 to 3 tablespoons of the jelly into a mug of hot water.
8. Let the tea steep for 3 minutes then enjoy.

Conclusion

After reading this book you should know everything you need to know about honey to get you started in using it as a natural herbal remedy. Not only have you learned about the long history of this substance but you have also received a long list of the benefits it can have for you and your family. If you are convinced that honey is indeed a magical healing substance, get to work in using some of the recipes provided in this book to start making your own natural remedies. Before you know it you will be emptying out your medicine cabinet and stocking up on honey!

About the Author

Amy Adams is a nutritionist and lover of ALL things healthy. You will find her practicing yoga every morning and attending a Pilates class twice a week. She loves cooking and only ever uses natural non-processed ingredients. She was taught to use natural and herbal remedies by her mother who doesn't agree with using antibiotics for common ailments. Her other book 'Natural Antibiotics' includes homemade natural herbal remedies for everyday illnesses, infections and allergies.